# BITING BACK:
# TACKLING REPEAT BURGLARY
# AND CAR CRIME

David Anderson
Sylvia Chenery
Ken Pease

POLICE RESEARCH GROUP
CRIME DETECTION AND PREVENTION SERIES: PAPER No 58
LONDON: HOME OFFICE POLICE DEPARTMENT

Editor: Barry Webb
Home Office Police Research Group
50 Queen Anne's Gate
London SW1H 9AT

Police Research Group: Crime Detection and Prevention Series

The Home Office Police Research group (PRG) was formed in 1992 to carry out and manage research relevant to the work of the police service. The terms of reference for the Group include the requirement to identify and disseminate good police practice.

The Crime Detection and Prevention Series follows on from the Crime Prevention Unit papers, a series which has been published by the Home Office since 1983. The recognition that effective crime strategies will often involve both crime prevention and crime investigation, however, has led to the scope of this series being  broadened. This new series will present research material on both crime prevention and detection in a way which informs policy and practice throughout the service.

A parrellel series of papers on resource management and organisational issues is also published by PRG, as is a periodical on policing research called 'Focus'.

ISBN     1-85893-343-9

# Foreword

The project which is the subject of this report has an important place in the Home Office programme of research and development on repeat victimisation. It marks a shift of focus going beyond one-off research projects, which have now clearly established the need to prevent repeat victimisation in the management of crime, to how the prevention of repeat victimisation could become part of routine policing practice.

Other events in 1994 have consolidated this shift. These include the National Board for Crime Prevention's repeat victimisation paper and regional conferences, the serious consideration being given to repeat victimisation as a performance indicator for the police and the announcement of the setting up of a repeat victimisation task force in the Home Office.

The purpose of this project is to see how far it is practical to expect forces to tackle repeat victimisation as part of their crime management strategies, and to provide guidance on how the current obstacles to this might be overcome. This report describes the first phase of work in Huddersfield, the research and events leading up to the launch of the strategy on 17th November 1994. A final report on the project, in which the problems and achievements of the strategy will be examined, is due at the end of 1995.

**IM BURNS**
*Deputy Under Secretary of State*
*Home Office, Police Department*
*December 1994*

# Acknowledgements

Thanks are due to so many people that omissions are inevitable. Those meriting particular thanks include Chief Superintendent Cornmell, Chief Superintendent Lloyd, Inspector Galvin and Mr. Homer at Force Headquarters. Gratitude is owed to Superintendent Alan Dobson and his staff at Huddersfield, particularly DCI John Holt (Divisional Crime Manager) and DS John Barr (Project Co-ordinator), Chief Inspector Jeff Denham, to Tony Elson, Sheila Collins and Cath Emery of Kirklees Metropolitan Council, to Pauline Goldthorpe and colleagues in Victim Support, to the members of the Special Constabulary who assisted in interviewing repeat victims, and to Paul Broadbent of Manchester Metropolitan University. We are grateful for support from Thatcham.

Thanks are due to Barry Webb, Cressida Bridgeman and Gloria Laycock of the Home Office Police Research Group for their unfailing help and encouragement.

The last thanks should go to all the police officers at Huddersfield. That such a group of experienced (and professionally sceptical) people has been open-minded enough to contribute ideas and effort to the approach is a source of gratitude and satisfaction.

## The Authors

David Anderson is a Police Inspector with the West Yorkshire force. In his twenty years service he has worked in a variety of roles, and is currently in the force's Research and Analysis Department.

Sylvia Chenery has been a social worker and market research interviewer. She has worked on repeat victimisation for a year, primarily on the Huddersfield project, but also on analysis of British Crime Survey data on series victimisations.

Ken Pease is Professor of Criminology at Manchester University and member of the National Board for Crime Prevention. He has worked intermittently on repeat victimisation for almost ten years.

# Executive summary

The report describes the process from conception to implementation of a project based in Huddersfield to reduce rates of burglary and vehicle crime (theft of and from motor vehicles) by concentrating on the prevention of repeated victimisation of the same target. The basic purpose of the project is to illustrate the means whereby the prevention of repeats could become a standard method of crime prevention delivery, and the problems and compromises involved in making the transition from a project-based approach to routine good practice.

The project confirmed previous research establishing that there were many repeat crimes, and that they tended to occur quickly after a prior offence. However, it identified that there were problems in always recognising repeats as such from the West Yorkshire force's Crime Information System. Although the system is very sophisticated, it was not set up with the identification of repeats as a primary concern. Difficulties in identifying repeats will prove a massive obstacle to the evaluation of programmes to prevent repeat victimisation, and to the consideration of that prevention as a performance indicator for the police service.

Research preparatory to the implementation in Huddersfield establishes the often crushing impact of repeat victimisation by domestic burglary on people's lives, the fact that repeat victims identified from crimes reported to the police constitute a substantial underestimate of their true rates of victimisation, and that the risk of repeat burglary of the same house is significantly higher than the risk of burglary of an adjacent house. Analysis of interviews with victims of other offence types is pending, and hopefully will yield still more information pertinent to the scheme's development.

The system developed in West Yorkshire takes prevention as an overarching purpose which can be achieved by either or both of the complementary methods of *deflection* from targets or *detection* of perpetrators. It grades responses according to the number of previous victimisations (as recounted by the victim) from bronze through silver to gold. The components of the response vary from the simple (like property marking and security uprating) through focused patrolling of victimised places, to the loan of high technology measures like vehicle tracking and silent alarms. The emphasis on detection increases with the number of prior victimisations and includes priority of previous victims for prompt fingerprint analysis and targeting of previous offenders against the same target. The precise composition of measures will vary with time, further research and experience. The scheme is a true partnership with the police, Victim Support, Kirklees Metropolitan Council and Huddersfield University all making tangible contributions. A report in late 1995 will detail the scheme's development and preventive effects.

# Contents

# List of Tables

# List of Figures

# 1. Background and beginnings

The project flowed from previous work funded by the Home Office Police Research Group on repeated crime victimisation, beginning with the Kirkholt Burglary Project of the mid-1980s (Forrester et al. 1988) and continuing with work on offences as diverse as domestic violence and racial attacks (see eg. Lloyd et al. 1994; Sampson and Phillips, 1992).

In sum, this work suggested that: victimisation is heavily concentrated upon particular individuals and places; areas with high crime rates are disproportionately characterised by high rates of repeat victimisation (Trickett et al. 1992); repeated victimisations tend to occur swiftly (Polvi et al. 1991), and such evidence as exists indicates that the same offenders may often be responsible (see eg. Chenery et al. 1994; Winkel, 1991).

The implications of this approach for crime prevention generally have been succinctly summarised in a report by the National Board for Crime Prevention (NBCP). In the conclusions section of the NBCP report, the project whose beginnings are described below is referred to as follows: "One example ... is the work underway in West Yorkshire, where the Home Office has commissioned Manchester University to work with West Yorkshire Police to develop strategies to tackle repeat domestic and commercial burglary and theft of and from motor vehicles." (Bridgeman and Sampson, 1994)

The project specification document contended that the proposed work represented the "means whereby the prevention of repeat victimisation moves from a technique shown to have been effective in one-off contexts to one capable of routine application by force CPOs. Prevention of repeat victimisation by all appropriate means would be the approach espoused. This kind of targeting has both preventive and crime solution benefits. Since the strong circumstantial evidence points to the same offenders being involved in repeated offences against the same targets, the targeting of victimised places or vehicles will *ipso facto* involve detections of repeated offenders".

The overall objectives of the project were:

1.  To reduce the probability of revictimisation among those suffering theft of or from motor vehicles.

2.  To reduce the probability of victimisation among those suffering burglary (domestic or commercial).

3.  To identify the advantages, problems and compromises involved in translating the prevention of repeat victimisation from a project-based technique to the standard mode of crime prevention delivery.

The West Yorkshire Police force area was nominated as the location for the two-year project. The force itself nominated the Huddersfield division as its precise site. This report describes the process whereby the project moved from conception to implementation. A later report will document developments during full implementation and any changes achieved by the project. While the police service is inevitably the lead agency, the active involvement of Kirklees Metropolitan Council and Victim Support makes this a partnership in substance as well as in name.

**Let no-one put asunder**

Experience in Huddersfield has been stimulating not only at the project level, but also in elaborating the way in which the prevention of repeats can be a cornerstone of crime control generally. The reader is asked to be tolerant of a few paragraphs given to the development of this theme, which seems to the writers to be of crucial importance.

Historically, two schisms in crime control and the treatment of victims have opened up. One separates crime prevention and victim support. The other divides crime prevention and offender detection. It is worth speculating whether either of these divisions would have occurred had the extent of repeat victimisation been recognised at the time when they took place.

*Crime prevention and victim support*

One of the virtues of preventing repeat victimisation as a general crime prevention strategy (stressed in the National Board publication) is the reconciliation of reactive and proactive responses to crime. Crime prevention and victim support are necessary for the *same* people (recent victims) at the *same* time (promptly after their victimisation). *Reaction* to the last offence, if it has a preventive element, is *proaction* to the next. Reaction to the last offence, if it has *no* preventive component, is useless in protecting crime victims, in that it leaves unprotected those most likely to be victimised in the future. Well-intentioned police officers and victim support volunteers have often comforted victims that, "lightning doesn't strike twice", or, "it will be someone else's turn next". While the motive is laudable and the content of the message is understandable, it is both factually wrong and forgoes the opportunity to implement preventive measures at the time when to do so has the greatest scope for preventing crime and assuaging the feelings of helplessness of the crime victim.

*Crime prevention and crime detection*

As for the schism between crime prevention and crime detection, experience in Huddersfield has emphasised how close these two functions can be. Indeed, since detection may prevent some future offences of the same perpetrator, detection is one prevention method. It may be that the vocabulary needs to be changed to make this inclusive-included status clearer. Perhaps we should think of prevention as the overarching aim of the police, which can be achieved by the parallel and complementary methods of crime *detection* and crime *deflection*. Often there is a subtle equipment choice which determines which of the functions is being served. For instance, installation of an intruder alarm aims at crime prevention through deflection if it is visible and audible, and at crime prevention through detection if it is covert and silent. CCTV aims at deflection if it is overt, and detection if covert and the tape is geared to evidentiary requirements. The equipment is essentially the same in both cases, but the route to crime prevention is different.

In the thinking of our collaborators in West Yorkshire and ourselves, the progression from an emphasis on deflection to one on detection as the number of repeats increases came almost automatically. Assuming the same offenders to be responsible for repeats, this will hopefully eliminate opportunist offenders by basic deflection techniques, leaving the more sophisticated detection techniques targeted on the numerically fewer frequent repeaters. Some indirect evidence from West Yorkshire that the same offenders are responsible for much repeat burglary is included in this report.

## Getting started

In September 1993, a preliminary meeting at force Headquarters took a number of decisions central to the project's development:

- Huddersfield should be the project site for the following reasons: there is a good relationship between the police and Kirklees Metropolitan Council; Huddersfield as a division is fairly typical of the others in the force area; and, other divisions in the area currently have substantial work being carried out in them, for example the Safer Cities work in Bradford, which could make evaluation of this project less straightforward.

- A police project manager should be nominated (the first author of this report).

- A steering group should be set up to oversee the project. This would be chaired by the police as lead agency, but would need to involve key local agencies, including the local authority and Victim Support. Representatives should be of sufficiently senior level to take decisions.

This established a framework for taking the project forward. The first year of the project has seen three overlapping phases: the research phase; strategy development, and strategy implementation. This is illustrated by figure 1. The following sections discuss each of these in more detail and outline future developments.

## Figure 1: The project diary - key dates

| | | |
|---|---|---|
| 17 September 1993 | Preliminary meeting | |
| 20 October 1993 | First meeting of the steering group | |
| 16 December 1993 | Steering group meeting | *RESEARCH PHASE* |
| 16 May 1994 | Steering group meeting | *(Chapter 2)* |
| 14 June 1994 | Management team meeting | |
| 20 June 1994 | Briefing task group leaders | |

*Task Group*

| | | |
|---|---|---|
| 17 August 1994 | Task group reports delivered to project manager | *STRATEGY DEVELOPMENT* |
| 2 September 1994 | Management team meeting to discuss options | *(Chapter 3)* |
| 5 September 1994 | Steering group meeting to approve implementation strategy. Project co-ordinator appointed. | |
| 26-30 September 1994 | Training sessions for all police officers concerned | |
| | | *STRATEGY IMPLEMENTATION (Chapter 4)* |
| **1 October 1994** | IMPLEMENTATION | |
| 17 November 1994 | Media launch | |

## 2. The research phase

This section describes the research phase of the project which involved detailed analysis of data from the force's Crime Information System (CIS). Interviews with repeat victims of the crime types under consideration were also conducted and these are discussed at the end of the section.

### Data collection

The first task was to gather data from the force's CIS, the anticipated source of most information on repeats, now and in the future. The idea was to download from the system relevant subsets of the data in ASCII format, which then could be analysed in more detail. For reasons which are explained in the next sub-section, the CIS could not be used itself to identify and analyse repeat victimisation fully. After some delay in gaining training and access to the system, a command was framed which would download all possible repeats.[1]

It also became clear that changing beat boundaries limited the period over which repeats could be studied to a maximum of eleven months. This is lower than the minimum recommended by Farrell and Pease (1993) but could not be helped.

Once the data had been downloaded, the process began of manually checking the data and converting it to a form which could be read into an SPSS system file for analysis. The work was massively time consuming. It took four months. This seems an inordinately long time in the context of the project as a whole and should be justified. Those willing to accept that there were difficulties and not interested in their nature should skip to the next sub-heading in this report.

The ASCII data files came with variable space lengths and occasional intrusive alphanumeric characters. There were some 8000 cases. Word Perfect macros were devised to eliminate these problems. This was itself not a straightforward process. For instance, month fields were converted from alphanumeric to numeric, with JAN becoming 01, and so on. It was only later that we realised how often Black and Decker tools had been stolen. The process by which DEC had been converted to 12 had also converted these tools to Black and 12ker tools.

1 There is agreement in principle to download a sample of single victimisations for comparison purposes in the future.

This process eliminated only around half of all the problems. Resolution of the remainder involved painstaking manual work, during which some of the inconsistencies of spelling were resolved. An SPSS/DE template was devised and the data fed in. This also was not straightforward. For example, sometimes an original coding comprised an O (capital o) rather than 0 (zero), which SPSS obviously rejected in a numeric field, making a semi-manual search necessary. During that time, a variety of problems emerged with the form of the CIS data which are important both for the conduct and evaluation of the project, and more widely for the incorporation of the counting of repeats into performance indicators and the like. These issues are outlined in the next section of the report.

**Lessons of the conversion process: the identification of repeats**

The CIS system in West Yorkshire is sophisticated in many ways. What follows is not intended to be critical of it, nor of the skilled and committed people who designed it and enter data into it. They have been helpful and supportive. The system was simply not designed or operated to fulfil the needs of this project. Conversations with those who have carried out equivalent analyses in other forces make it clear that the scope for identifying repeats in West Yorkshire is certainly no less than in most other forces, and is probably greater. The problems we faced are a product of the historical indifference to identifying repeat victimisation.

For most matters of practical policing, even those which recognise the importance of repeat victimisation, the problems identified below are not serious, primarily because a police officer can always ask questions of a complainant to clarify a position. They do, however, present serious obstacles to the reliable measurement and monitoring of repeat victimisation.

A CIS entry is completed for every event classified as a crime. The police officer attending the scene communicates with a clerk in the CIS Bureau, who enters details of the crime. The sophistication of CIS is clear. For instance, it makes it difficult for an operator recording a crime to mis-spell street names by offering a set of alternatives to an unrecognised street name, and gives a choice of districts where the same street name occurs in more than one. If the unique identification of an address were simply a matter of street number and street name, and there was no confusion about the district in which a particular dwelling fell, then there would be little room for confusion about which place-specific events (like burglary) were single and which repeat events.[2]

2 There would still be some. Some flexibility is obviously necessary so that crime in new or renamed streets can be included. Thus it is possible (and has occurred) for crime entry to override a correctly spelled street with an incorrectly spelled street.

*Identifying repeat burglary*

Problems were least substantial for the offence of domestic burglary. So far, three fields in the CIS system have been discussed. These are street number, street name and district. Typically, this means that houses which are not subdivided and which are identified by numbers alone, and where a street number is entered in the relevant field, should be clearly identifiable as once or repeatedly victimised. However, this leaves three problem areas:

1. Houses which are identified by name rather than number;

2. Houses with a common number but which are subdivided into flats; and,

3. Houses without a recorded name or number.

These situations cause problems because the look-up facility for street names does not extend to individual dwellings. This is scarcely surprising, since to do so would be a major undertaking. In practice, it means that another field, the 'feature' field, must be examined in some detail. This field often (but not always) identifies flat, house name (with non-standardised spellings) or sometimes something different, eg 'back of'. In short, there is a penumbra of uncertainty even about the extent of domestic burglary repeats. Such problems are much greater in respect of other burglaries and of motor vehicle crime. Whereas dwellings are typically identified by number, most other places are not. The possible confusion in the feature field is immense. Many different spellings exist for the most victimised places.

*Identifying repeat vehicle crime*

A central concern of the project is the prevention of thefts of and from motor vehicles. Quantifying repeats here is intrinsically more complex, and merits a slight digression before the problems of CIS identification of vehicle crime repeats are described.

A vehicle crime repeat could be defined in at least three ways:

1. Any vehicle, anywhere, from the same complainant;

2. Any vehicle from the same location irrespective of its owner;

3. The same vehicle from any location even across changes of owner.

For reasons which were largely pragmatic, we chose the third. Complainant details had not been requested from CIS, so option 1 was impracticable. Option 2, which includes as repeats *different* cars stolen from the same location makes repeat victimisation equivalent to a hot spot, and does not require action directed to a particular victimised vehicle. To go down this route would have complicated our intervention strategy, and in any event this would not have been possible given the imprecision with which location of vehicle theft was typically recorded, eg. is "Webb Street", and "outside 14 Webb Street" the same place? It is worth noting, however, that such a definition would be the one most consistent with our approach to dwellings. Dwellings are locations so that in the prevention approach adopted at Kirkholt and elsewhere, it is the locations that are protected, not the property found at those locations. By analogy, car parks would be protected, not the transient contents of the car park. Analysing at the level of individual vehicles in locations is rather like analysing at the level of individual stealable items in a house or shop.

Option 3, which looks at individual motor vehicles regardless of location or owner, was thus chosen by default, and also because it was thought to offer the best chance of getting accurate levels of repeat victimisation. In practice, there is a substantial coincidence between location and individual vehicle, with over half of all theft involving cars taking place around the home (Mayhew et al. 1993).

Having rehearsed the possible definitions of repeats involving vehicles, we now return to the practical difficulties of identifying them using the CIS. Many cases were found where cars stolen from the same place have Vehicle Registration Marks (VRMs) which differ by only one letter or number, and more where the differences were only slightly greater. Because the name and address of the complainant were not extracted, it proved impossible at the time to undertake even a partial check on which of these were true repeats.[3] However, our feeling is that in the bulk of these cases errors in transmission of the VRM are responsible for the differences, thus greatly understating the extent of identified repeats.

**The lesson of our experience with CIS for the project, and particularly for its evaluation, is that there is no easy way of measuring change in the proportion of repeat victimisations with any precision.** The closest estimates can be made in relation to domestic burglary. Any attempt to measure police performance by the use of repeat offences relies upon the reasonably accurate identification of repeats. Our conclusion (consistent with

3 *What is now envisaged is a return to the CIS system with our SPSS file, to see if there are any fields to which we did not have access which would clarify the status of a victimisation as a repeat or otherwise.*

that of Tilley communicated informally to us) is that this cannot routinely be done from most current police crime information systems, even more sophisticated systems like that operated in West Yorkshire.

The problem of identifying repeats in police records is immense. However, the limited extent to which police have repeat offences reported to them makes this pale into relative insignificance. In our interview study of those who had reported more than one offence to the police, one concern was to clarify the number of offences which repeat victims had suffered, and to see how that compared with the number they had reported to the police. Some preliminary indication of this is presented towards the end of this section.

In passing, it is worth noting that non-report is one of the reasons why the scale of repeat victimisation is understated in the experience of police officers. Other reasons are that their experience of a particular area tends to be fragmented by shift changes, the intrusion of other functions, illness, holidays and the like.

### Results of preliminary analysis

The principal reason for undertaking an analysis of CIS data was to determine the approximate extent and time course of repeat victimisation. The picture will be assessed offence by offence.

Table 1 illustrates for each offence category: the number of offences recorded; the number of these which could be repeats; and, the number which are definite repeats.

| Table 1: The extent of repeat victimisation in Huddersfield | | | | |
|---|---|---|---|---|
| | Domestic burglary | Commercial burglary | Theft of motor vehicle | Theft from a motor vehicle |
| Number recorded | 3951 | 2144 | 3116 | 4891 |
| Possible repeats | 927 (23.5%) | 1490 (69.5%) | 1518 (49%) | 2727 (56%) |
| Definite repeats | 623 (16%) | 597 (28%) | 181 (6%) | 484 (10%) |

For domestic burglary, 3951 offences were recorded during the eleven-month period under consideration in the relevant police subdivision. Of these, 927 (23.5%) were putative repeats. However, many of these were included because of missing data in certain fields, which made it impossible to be clear about their status. There were an absolute minimum of 623 offences (16%) suffered by dwellings which were definite targets of more than one offence in the time period.

For commercial burglary, 2144 offences were recorded in the area during the period in question. Of these 1490 (69.5%) were putative repeats. A total of 597 (28%) offences were unequivocal repeats. This number will be massively increased after simple editing of the data file (eg. making Ashbrow School match with Ash Brow school).

For theft/taking of motor vehicles, 3116 offences were recorded by the police, of which 1518 (49%) came to us as putative repeats. The absolute minimum number of certain repeats (thefts of the same vehicle) was 181 (6%).

For theft from a motor vehicle, 4891 were recorded, 2727 (56%) came to us as putative repeats, and 484 (10%) were unequivocal repeats.

Two points could be addressed to be consistent with our approach in earlier projects. First, are these minimum numbers in line with what one would expect if the events were independent, ie. are these numbers of repeats more or less what we would expect given the amount of crime and the number of potential targets in the area? This particular measurement issue is discussed more fully in Tilley (1995). This will not be analysed in the present report, because the results would be misleading at least until we have clarified the status of events as repeats or otherwise. Even then, it will be possible to address it only in relation to domestic burglary and vehicle crime, as it would be very difficult to ascertain the number of premises in the area which, if burgled, would be classified as burglary (other).

The second point concerns whether the time course of repeat victimisation describes the curve which is familiar from previous research, ie. levels of risk as time elapses from a prior victimisation. The short answer is that it did, for all crime types of concern. Figures 2-5 show the time course curves for domestic burglary, other burglary, theft of and theft from motor vehicles, indicating that repeat victimisation across all these crime types takes place soon after a prior victimisation. Appendix A provides a more detailed methodological note on the analysis and presentation of this time course data.

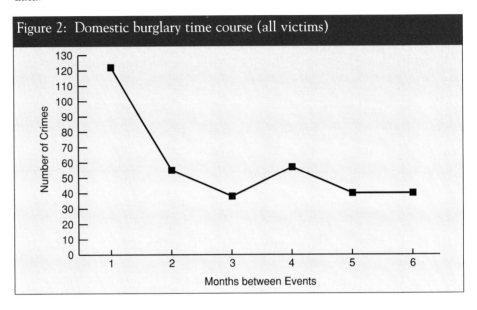

Figure 2: Domestic burglary time course (all victims)

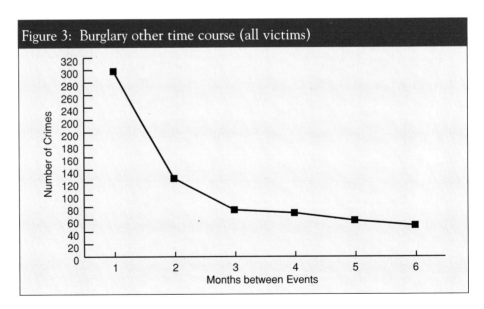

Figure 3: Burglary other time course (all victims)

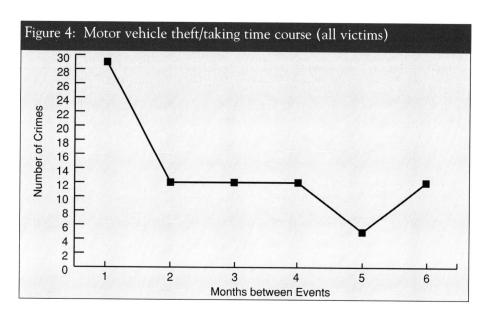

Figure 4: Motor vehicle theft/taking time course (all victims)

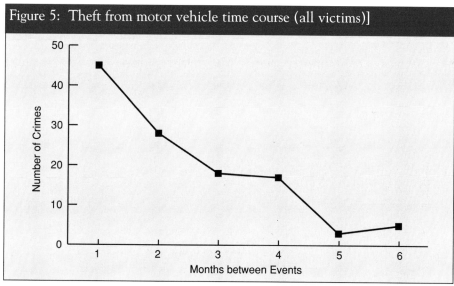

Figure 5: Theft from motor vehicle time course (all victims)]

## Interviews with repeat domestic burglary victims

As noted earlier, interviews with repeat victims were undertaken. These were repeat victims of domestic burglary, repeat victims of other burglary, victims of vehicle-related offences, and victims of a mixture of vehicle-related offences and burglary. In this section, interviews with victims of domestic burglary are superficially reported. They will be subject to more formal analysis. 266 addresses were randomly selected for interview. The only similarity between the cases was that they had all been victims of at least two burglaries at this address between January 1st and November 30th 1993. Of this number, 84 interviews have been completed.

The main reasons for the other multiple domestic burglary victims not being interviewed were that people had moved away, died or the interviewer was unable to gain a response after a minimum of two attempts. Also, some burglaries of commercial premises had been miscoded on CIS as burglaries of dwellings. The interviews took place during April-July 1994. In what follows, attempts are included as burglaries.

*Information from interviews*

From the 84 households interviewed, 262 burglaries were recalled. Thus there were around 3.1 per household over the recall period of (on average) seventeen months. Of these, only 2.1 were said to have been reported to the police. Thus the number of burglaries in police records for this group would have to be increased by some 50% to reflect the level of burglaries suffered.

Another way of looking at the data is that since the eleven-month period which identified these people as repeat victims, a further 50 burglaries had been suffered. This confirms two points. First, the group identified as repeats by police records was actually victimised more often than those records show. Second, their victimisation persisted beyond the period which defined them as repeat victims.

These data indicate that nearly 200 burglaries could have been prevented if each interviewed victim had been effectively protected after the first offence. If their experience was typical of those whom we were unable to interview the figure would be nearly 600 for the sample. This is likely to be an underestimate of the amount of repeat victimisation open to prevention by this project; since the strategy will cover repeat victims not currently identified as such by the CIS, and since the period studied for these calculations was only eleven months.

*Domestic burglary patterns*

The interview concentrated on the time distribution of burglaries in more detail than known victimisation surveys in the past. The familiar time course reasserts itself in this data set, with some 40% of all repeats taking place within a month of the preceding one.

Windows were the point of entry in over two-thirds of both completed and attempted burglaries. Clearly window security must feature in the programme of work to be undertaken. The house was unoccupied at the time of the offence in two-thirds of cases. Items most frequently taken were videos, TVs, CD/stereo systems and other electronic goods. Together one or more of these items were taken in 64% of cases.

A very important question for the project is how wide-ranging the project actions should be. So far, analysis has concentrated on same type repeats. However, the households interviewed had, over the recall period covered, also suffered other offences. Forty-five percent had suffered one or more thefts from a motor vehicle, and 15% theft/taking of a motor vehicle.

Where comments on the interview schedule have been made on position of house, it is interesting to see how many properties have a secluded rear or side paths/alleyways. It may be that attention to security lighting of entry points to the house from these may form part of the project.

Further analysis of the interview data will be undertaken in due course to show similarity of entry points, time sequences between attempts and completions to the same dwelling, awareness of offender characteristics, and the like.

*Impact of repeated burglary on quality of life*

Read about in research reports, or otherwise distanced from personal emotions, repeat victimisation can be regarded as an interesting phenomenon with crime prevention implications. Interviewing repeat victims brings one face-to-face with the effects such victimisation has upon people's lives. A few case descriptions follow, to illustrate this.

Case 1
Young family in new private property - burgled once and suffered two attempts. Wife has been unable to sleep at night and for some time refused to leave the house. She is still very worried whenever she has to leave the home.

Case 2
Two burglaries have had a significant effect on this elderly couple. The wife has since suffered two strokes, which she and her husband link to the upset of the burglaries, and she is now totally reliant on her husband to take care of her and is unable to leave the home. Talking about the incidents still distresses her. Following the second incident, the husband (in his 70's) slept upright in the sitting room chair, facing the window where they had gained entry, holding an iron bar and a torch. The idea was that if they tried to get in he would shine the torch into their faces and if that failed to chase them away he would hit them with the bar.

Case 3
This family feels victimised by its insurance company. Following two burglaries the insurance company raised its premium by 30%, and refused to cover them at all unless the occupants had an alarm installed. This they did, but as the wife could not sleep, fearful of every noise, they sold their house and bought another in a different area (one much less prone to burglaries). This house has every security device they can think of but still the insurance company would not reduce their premiums. They have tried to insure with other companies who refuse to insure them at all.

Case 4
This retired couple moved to a bungalow with a nice garden at the rear, overlooking playing fields. The husband particularly wanted to buy this so he could watch all the sporting activities going on behind his house. Not long after moving in they had their first burglary. Entry was made by the patio door, so they purchased a new door (stronger than the first). Entry was again made by the patio door, so they purchased an alarm. Burglars attempted to gain entry again through this door and were stopped only because they were disturbed. The couple then purchased a 'tremble' alarm connected to the patio doors. This was so sensitive that even when the glass was touched the alarm was triggered. The garage was broken into - so they built a new garage. A front window was attacked - so they changed all the windows to small top opening ones. The side door was attacked - so they purchased a new 7 lever lock door. The house is now like (to quote)

Fort Knox, but the offenders, not to be outdone, stole the satellite dish from the roof! Most of their savings that the victims expected to spend on a comfortable retirement have now gone. The police obviously recognised a problem, and promised the loan of a 'silent' alarm, connected to the station- however, up to the time of this interview the victims had not received this.

Case 5

This couple have had two burglaries, a number of attempts, and a number of acts of damage committed to their home. This resulted in the husband having a nervous breakdown. They feel their problems all started when they observed the Post Office opposite their home being burgled. They phoned the police who responded quickly, but came to their home giving the culprits the chance to see who had 'shopped' them. Two were caught, one escaped, but life has not been the same for the family since. They blame the police for not being discreet.

*Domestic burglary and car theft: some sequences*

The sequences of victimisation of different types deserve more scrutiny. One of us in interviews got the feeling that theft of cars tended to follow domestic burglary at the same address, presumably because the absence of spare car keys was not noticed, or because documentation was taken which allowed duplicate keys to be obtained. The hypothesis was generated that where both offences were suffered at the same address, it would be the burglary that was suffered first. Further, it was guessed that the time between the offences would be shorter when the burglary came first than when the car theft came first.

Both hypotheses proved to be unfounded. There were precisely as many households where the car theft came first as where the burglary came first. The average time between events was the same in both directions of sequence.

However, before the ideas of linkage are totally rejected, it should be noted that there were as many as 80 addresses where both offences were suffered.[4] Whether this simply reflects area differences, or whether there are links between these offence types is a matter for determination. The interviews to be undertaken with 'mixed' victims will hopefully clarify matters.

4 *Analysis of expected rates of combination will be carried out once we know the size of the car population of the area.*

*Interviews with repeat victims of vehicle crime*

Fifty such interviews have been conducted. These are not yet in a state for full analysis, but it is clear that the offences occur mainly outside the home, between 10pm and 5am. Thefts of visible personal property and radio-cassettes predominate. Under-reporting to the police is substantial, and apparently reporting to the insurance companies is still less. "The scrap yards of Huddersfield [are] doing a roaring trade in front near side windows, quarterlights, and locks."

# 3. From data to action

The analysis of data undertaken and described above had three results. It persuaded the relevant officers in West Yorkshire police and the Manchester project staff that:

1. The West Yorkshire data systems provided substantial or massive underestimates of the extent of repeat victimisation.

2. Notwithstanding the fact that the data captured underestimated repeat victimisation, its absolute amount was such as to merit attention.

3. The time course of repeats was such as to justify giving priority to *prompt* preventive action in relation to recent victims.

Having established a basis on which action could be justified, the next stage was to move the project towards action. A background paper was prepared by the research team. This set out a range of intervention possibilities which could be considered. A meeting of the project steering group was held and a framework was established within which the project was to be advanced. This is depicted as figure 6.

**Figure 6: Project management structure**

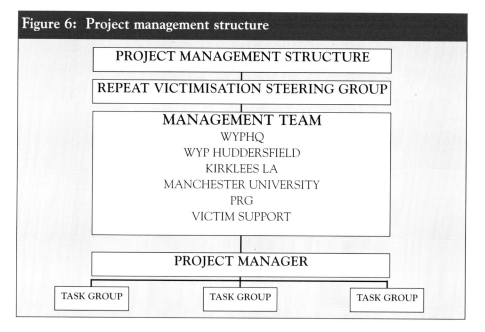

A management team was set up, responsible to the steering group, with membership from the Home Office Police Research Group, West Yorkshire Police, Kirklees Metropolitan Council, Victim Support and Manchester University, and meeting regularly. Reporting to the group and in administrative charge was the Project Manager, the first author of this report.

### The task groups

Three task groups were established. One was to take forward the introduction of a Geographic Information System for crime pattern analysis in West Yorkshire which would incorporate a facility for the better identification of repeat victimisations. This was under the Chairmanship of Inspector John Leithley. The division of work between the second and third task groups was novel, and its origins merit extended mention.

In his doctoral dissertation, Farrell (1993) linked the phenomena of repeat victimisation to routine activity theory (see Cohen and Felson 1979). According to this theory, three elements must coincide for a crime to occur. These are:
- a motivated offender;
- a suitable victim;
- the absence of a capable guardian.

The idea that a crime can be prevented by removing any one of these three essential elements is breathtakingly simple, but defines the entire repertoire of crime prevention methods. This way of thinking about crime and crime prevention was presented at the regional conferences on repeat victimisation organised by the NBCP (Laycock, 1994) and stuck in the minds at least of the West Yorkshire officers who attended. It consequently turned out to offer the preferred method of organising task groups to move the Huddersfield Project towards action.

Two ways of organising task groups were considered. One was to deal with all means of reducing a particular crime type, so that there would be one task group for burglary and one for motor crime. The alternative was to classify by the means of reducing repeats. Figure 7 illustrates the two alternatives of organising the task groups either horizontally or vertically.

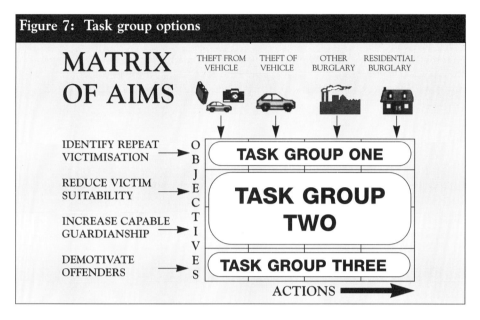

Figure 7: Task group options

MATRIX OF AIMS

Discussion indicated that the horizontal approach, whereby the groups are subdivided to deal with one term of routine activity theory each, was to be preferred. It had two particular advantages. First, it allowed a clearer view of what the membership of the groups should be. Second, it concentrated discussion on the mechanisms of crime prevention. It has been persuasively argued (for instance by Pawson and Tilley, 1994) that an emphasis on mechanism is essential for the development and the evaluation of crime prevention programmes. This way of approaching the task offered some protection against the conventional thinking of what one does in response to burglary or vehicle crime, and it was hoped would generate some innovative ideas.

One task group was thus given the responsibility of devising ways of demotivating offenders, and the second was given the responsibility for devising ways of decreasing victim suitability and increasing capable guardianship. These two elements of routine activities theory were combined in the work of one group because they seemed to be rather similar. It was felt that victim suitability was defined as the absence of capable guardianship, either because the victim him/herself was incapable of exercising guardianship, or because neighbours and others seemed little in evidence. Cohen and Felson (1979) also place the same two elements in an overlapping relationship.

### A graded response

The membership of the three task groups was decided at a project management group meeting, and a subsequent meeting of task group leaders determined the basic framework for the strategy. This was the notion of a graded response to victimisation depending upon the number of prior victimisations. These were to be described in shorthand terms as bronze, silver and gold responses.

The bronze response was the least ambitious, and could therefore be widely used. The silver response was to be intermediate, and the gold response was to comprise a relatively high-tech package restricted to the most victimised places. **At its simplest, the bronze response would follow a first victimisation, the silver a second, and the gold a third.**

The advantage of the bronze-silver-gold characterisation was that it encapsulated the idea of graded response in a familiar way, and this way of describing things has caught on amongst the officers concerned. In the informal discussions in advance of the task groups, it was contended that the bronze-gold progression would also tend to be a progression from deflection of offenders to detection of offenders as the means of prevention.

### Estimation of numbers of golds, silvers and bronzes

In order to assess the practicality of responses to victimisation, it was important to calculate the numbers of bronzes, silvers and golds which would be generated. This is not as simple as it sounds. What follows is very imprecise, but illustrates the thinking required in developing this strategy and some of the problems encountered and assumptions made.

There are three basic implementation options, each of which generates quite different estimates of the number of bronze, silver and gold options which would be required. If a victim says that she has suffered three offences of the type during the preceding year, but none during the term of the project, is she allocated:

a: the bronze option, on the basis that hitherto no protection has been in place; any further victimisation during the first year of the project being allocated silver and gold in turn;

b: the gold option only, on the basis that she has suffered three prior victimisations in the preceding year;

c: the elements of all three options, on the basis that if she were offered only the gold option, the bronze and silver options would be lacking, making for less good protection.

Some numbers were calculated from West Yorkshire police records, but as noted earlier, these provide only a very partial view of the number of repeats. This would matter less if the information on the basis of which a response were to be allocated was police information, but it is not. As noted above, by far the most practicable means of deciding on the appropriate level of protection is by asking the victim how many times he/she has fallen victim to the offence in the preceding year. Thus offences hitherto unreported to the police will be used to decide the level of response, which makes the police data much less useful in calculating probable numbers of bronze, silver and gold responses required.

As the best alternative available, national data from the British Crime Survey (BCS) were used to get an idea of the numbers of gold, silver and bronze responses likely to be necessary. This data set allows the inclusion of unreported crimes which would be communicated to an officer asking the relevant question in the Huddersfield scheme as currently envisaged. For burglary other than domestic, there was no alternative to using West Yorkshire Police data, while knowing that this would represent an understatement of the real levels of gold and silver responses required.

There are difficulties in using BCS data to calculate the figures that need to be acknowledged. Let us assume that people become victims (ie. suffer a first victimisation) at a constant rate throughout the year. That means, in a calendar year, that half of the victims become victims in the first half of the year, and half become victims in the second half of the year. The average (median) date for first victimisation would be June 30th. Let us concentrate on this median victim, because she/he will have the average risk period for second victimisations. This 'average victim', the person whose first victimisation in the calendar year came on June 30th, has only six months in which to become a repeat victim.

In short, while the rate of *first* victimisation is based on a risk period of one year, the rate of *second* victimisation is based on a risk period of six months. One could continue the simplified description to conclude that the rate of *third* victimisations is based upon a risk period of three months, and of *fourth* victimisations is based upon a risk period of a mere six weeks.

The conclusion from this is that the proportion of silver and gold options which will in practice be required in Huddersfield is understated by the British Crime Survey data. The imprecision of the dating of events in that Survey makes it impossible to be confident about the amount of that underestimation. Offsetting this problem is the fact that we hope bronze level protection will work, reducing the number and proportion of gold and silver level options which are required.

Tables 2-4 summarise the estimates, based upon British Crime Survey data with the exception of non-domestic burglary, which is based upon West Yorkshire Police data, and which will also represent a substantial underestimate of the number of silver and gold options. The tables detail the outset and steady state numbers per 100 crimes of the type to which the police are called. The steady state options illustrated are identical, although they would differ insofar as the scheme was more or less successful than envisaged.

In all the estimates that follow, it is assumed that the effectiveness of the bronze level response will precisely offset the underestimation of rates of repeat victimisation in the British Crime Survey. If this is optimistic, the proportion and number of silver and gold responses will be greater. If it is pessimistic, the proportion and number of higher level responses will be smaller. No account has been taken of the differential effectiveness of gold relative to silver and silver relative to bronze options, because once again these are offset by the fact that the higher options go into higher risk places.

At 1993 rates, 100 domestic burglaries will occur in nine days, 100 other burglaries will occur in sixteen days, 100 thefts from a motor vehicle will occur in seven days, and 100 thefts/takings of motor vehicles will occur in eleven days. Put another way, at 1993 rates, over forty relevant offences occurred each day of the year. This gives an indication of the scale of the operation envisaged, and probably of the necessary modesty of the bronze option. *However*, insofar as the scheme is successful, the necessary scale should diminish, making the present enterprise a good candidate for special funding.

*Option a*          *The victim gets bronze, silver and gold successively for victimisations after the start of the project, irrespective of experience in the preceding months. The first victimisation of its type after the scheme onset evokes a bronze response, the second a silver, and the third a gold.*

In this scenario, virtually all the options in the first months of the scheme will be bronze, and those that will not will be silver. By the end of the first year, for every 100 domestic burglaries reported, 86 will require a bronze response, 12 will require silver, and 2 gold. The other offences are estimated in table 2.

**Table 2: Implementation option a: estimates of numbers of required bronze, silver and gold options, on day 1 and after one year of operation (per hundred offences)**

|  | Day | One |  | One | Year | On |
|---|---|---|---|---|---|---|
| Offence | Bronze | Silver | Gold | Bronze | Silver | Gold |
| Domestic burglary | 100 | 0 | 0 | 86 | 12 | 2 |
| Other burglary | 100 | 0 | 0 | 81 | 14 | 5 |
| Theft from mv | 100 | 0 | 0 | 77 | 17 | 6 |
| Theft/take mv | 100 | 0 | 0 | 90 | 8 | 2 |

*Option b*                    *Gold, silver or bronze protection is allocated on the basis of the prior year's victimisation. Lower level protection is not incorporated for those victims appearing for the first time in the project period, but who had been victims in the previous year.*

In this option, the proportion of higher level responses will be high at the start, and will revert to levels similar to those for option a after a year, as the preventive effect of bronze responses takes effect. The first half of table 3 is calculated by multiplying up the British Crime Survey estimates to compensate for diminishing risk periods on the lines set out earlier. The estimate for other burglary, being based on police data rather than British Crime Survey data, is not subject to a change on this basis.

**Table 3: Implementation option b: estimates of numbers of required bronze, silver and gold options, on day 1 and after one year of operation (per hundred offences)**

| | Day | One | | One | Year | On |
|---|---|---|---|---|---|---|
| Offence | Bronze | Silver | Gold | Bronze | Silver | Gold |
| Domestic burglary | 72 | 17 | 11 | 86 | 12 | 2 |
| Other burglary | 81 | 14 | 5 | 81 | 14 | 5 |
| Theft from mv | 57 | 22 | 21 | 77 | 17 | 6 |
| Theft/take mv | 80 | 12 | 8 | 90 | 8 | 2 |

| Option c | Gold, *silver or bronze protection is allocated on the basis of the prior year's victimisation, and lower level protection is incorporated for those victims appearing for the first time in the project period, but who had been victims in the previous year.* |

It will be noted that the numbers in table 4 add up to more than 100, as would self-evidently be the case if an offence triggered more than one level of response. It is clear that option c is by far the most resource-intensive of the three options. Against that, it is correspondingly the swiftest way of generating a general level of protection and producing a crime-reductive effect.

**Table 4: Implementation option c: estimates of numbers of required bronze, silver and gold options, on day 1 and after one year of operation (per hundred offences)**

| Offence | Day | One | | One | Year | On |
|---|---|---|---|---|---|---|
| | Bronze | Silver | Gold | Bronze | Silver | Gold |
| Domestic Burglary | 100 | 28 | 11 | 86 | 12 | 2 |
| Other Burglary | 100 | 19 | 5 | 81 | 14 | 5 |
| Theft from mv | 100 | 43 | 21 | 77 | 17 | 6 |
| Theft/take mv | 100 | 20 | 8 | 90 | 8 | 2 |

Each option generates quite different estimates of the number of bronze, silver and gold options which would be required. The right choice between these three alternatives is not self-evident. The decision taken has been a modified version of b, wherein the gold option is supplemented by bronze and silver elements deemed necessary to make protection real. If option a were chosen, officers would not quickly get into the notion of a progression. If option c were chosen, the scheme may become impossibly resource-intensive in its first year of operation.

Therefore, despite its acknowledged problems, notably resource demands early in the scheme, the modified option b is favoured.

# 4. The plan in action

In the briefing paper to the task groups, three issues were highlighted:

"1. The output of the groups should be in the form of specific actions to be triggered by an offence, and suggestions about the best organisational means of putting them into effect.

2. You should not exclude suggestions because you think the equipment is too costly or even because you don't know that it exists.

3. There is an overlap between the groups, and we are anxious that nothing falls into the gaps. We can cope with duplicate suggestions but we can't recreate them where each group has thought they fall within the province of the other group. For example, routine fingerprinting of a car after a theft from it is obviously relevant to demotivate (deter or detect) offenders, and will be considered by that group. The protection of a recovered car up to SS/PACT standards is obviously a way of reducing victim suitability/ installing a capable electronic guardian, and will be considered by that group. However, targeted patrolling, silent alarms etc. are arguably both. If an idea can have an effect by the mechanism to be covered by the group, we would like the group to consider it."

There was no dissent from the general principles underlying the project in either group. The issues which caused most contention were as follows:

1. The possible involvement of insurance companies raised anxiety. Several members felt uneasy with the idea of using insurer pressure to lever preventive measures into place. Others saw it as a necessary means of advancing the project.

2. There was concern about the dubious entitlement of a victim to a silver response if the components of the bronze response had not been installed or used properly.

3. There was concern that victims may be reluctant to relinquish loaned equipment after the loan period (the existence of a heightened risk period after victimisation has been documented in both this and previous work on repeat victimisation, and suggests scope for loaning equipment to victims over this period).

Apart from these three concerns, the meetings were characterised by much enthusiasm, goodwill, and ingenuity in deciding on the components of the package. There was a whole range of ideas. These varied from a lesson in how to remove a rotor arm as part of a bronze response to vehicle taking, to focused patrolling of the homes of recently burgled victims and forensic examination of car instrument cowls as part of the silver response, to Microdot protection of cars as part of a gold response.

Table 5 sets out the plan and initial raft of measures as of October 14th 1994.

| Table 5: Measures by offence type and level | | | |
|---|---|---|---|
| Offence | Bronze | Silver | Gold |
| All | Victim letter<br>Postcode pen<br>Informants check<br>Early check known outlets<br>Target offenders<br>CP advice | Victim letter<br>Search warrant<br>Micro-dots<br>Insurance incentives | Victim letter<br>Priority AFR<br>RV used for RIC<br>TrakBak<br>CCTV + video<br>High-tech devices as individually appropriate |
| Burglary | Rapid repair + security uprating<br>Victim support<br>Cocoon watch (dwellings only) | CPO visit and advice<br>Police Watch (min twice weekly)<br>'Police Aware' stickers<br>Mock occupancy devices, audible or dummy alarm, lighting, roller shutters | HO alarm<br>Police Watch (min daily)<br>Extended staff coverage (Burglary other) |
| Vehicle Crime | Vehicle Watch + U25 scheme<br>Early liaison with recovery location<br>Recover damaged cowling for SOCO<br>Car checks - self-help scheme<br>Window etching<br>Lease incentive scheme | Car check, car leaflets<br>Thatcham protection<br>Driveway barriers | CPO visit and advice<br>Laminated windows<br>Special number plates<br>SOCO |

*NB. As stressed in the text, this is certain to change with time and circumstances. Indeed, what is presented above is the last set of options mandated by the management group, and practice is already moving beyond this.*

The elements of the package which are not self-evident will be taken in turn.

**Bronze**

*The victim letter*

A personalised letter will be sent to each victim of crime indicating what actions will be taken by the police, and what actions should be taken by the victim. A postcode pen will be enclosed, the victim being invited to property mark, with the postcode, items of value in both home and vehicle. Stickers for display to indicate that postcoding has taken place will be enclosed.

*Early check known outlets*

Local field intelligence officers visit second hand dealers, pawn shops etc daily. It is not thought that they can visit car boot sales regularly.

*Cocoon watch*

As used in the Kirkholt Project (Forrester et al. 1988) this is an extension of house-to-house visits after a domestic burglary. Here, the neighbour is invited to look out for the victimised dwelling for the next few weeks, and is told that special measures are being taken to prevent it being victimised again. To the objection that the immediate neighbour may have been the burglar, this is seen as an advantage, with the offender being alerted to changed circumstances. If a neighbour is out when a call is made, information is left. The card asks for information about the last burglary and continues: "To assist your neighbour in feeling less vulnerable we would like to request your assistance and ask you to keep a 'watchful eye' on this property and if you see or hear anything suspicious please contact us immediately". This element of the scheme is obviously conditional upon the victim's consent. It falls short of the Kirkholt cocoon watch in that neighbours are not themselves offered security uprating, both because this would massively increase the resources needed to implement the bronze option, and because of the evidence about the levels of neighbour risk after a burglary contained in this report.

*Vehicle watch / under 25 schemes*

In these well-known schemes, the car bears decals indicating, respectively, that it is not usually out after midnight and is not legitimately driven by someone younger than 25.

*Early liaison with recovery location*

Where a car is recovered within the Division, this will ensure that there is no further damage or theft. When recovery is effected outside the division, this will ensure that crime patterns relevant to the division are identified.

*Recover damaged cowling for SOCO*

A damaged steering cowling is particularly suitable for fingerprint examination, and it will be removed for this purpose.

*Car checks and self-help scheme*

Identified 'hot spot' areas will be visited by a team of officers (possibly using Specials) at identified high risk times. Organisations like Hospital/Sports Centre will be invited to participate in checking car parks.

*CP advice*

This will start with the first visit or telephone record by the reporting officer. Later advice and leaflets will be contained in the personalised letter described earlier. At silver level the Crime Prevention Officer will visit.

**Silver**

*Search warrant*

A system for standardising police response to a victimisation based on previously detected offences is put into place. It will be dictated by a number of factors including similarity of property stolen and *modus operandi* to the offence reported here. The police response will range from heightened offender targeting for offences committed up to one year before the offence responded to under this project, to the possibility of arrest and PACE search for repeat offences where the offender is currently on bail.

This approach will also be taken for repeat offences committed up to eighteen months after the original, but where the offender was released from custody during the previous seven days.[5] The important change is that a formal structure now exists whereby information about previous offenders is used on every occasion, and with immediate action where appropriate.

*Microdots*

This is a sophisticated procedure so far used exclusively for vehicle theft but which can in principle be used for other items; an extension we are urgently seeking. In its vehicle application, all major components are sprayed with barely visible Microdots revealing the identity of the vehicle from which it comes. An offender cannot hope to locate more than a fraction of the Microdots without specialised equipment, so the components' origin can always be determined. A vehicle so marked is less attractive for ringing or for stripping into its individual components.

*'Police Watch'*

This is another measure generated by serving officers. It is a form of focused patrolling whereby a premises is visited at least twice per week during the six weeks after an offence during the time envelope when the original offence occurred. This has the dual purpose of increasing the likelihood that a patrolling officer is in the location of a crime being committed, and also that the officer is in a position to remind or encourage people to install any equipment recommended at the previous offence, if this has not happened.

*Car check*

In and around the place where cars have been victimised at this level, visits will be made by a team of officers (possibly using Specials) at identified high risk times. Where locations are attached to places like hospitals or sports centres, their staff will be invited to participate in checking car parks.

*Car leaflets*

Any communication with people whose vehicles have been found insecure will be individual. However, consideration will be given to flooding vehicles at the location with car security leaflets, which may contain general information about levels of car insecurity in the area.

5 *This is an instance of how local officers contributed to the scheme's development. During one of the training sessions, an experienced detective noted two different cases in which an offender's release had been closely followed by the revictimisation of houses previously hit just before he had been imprisoned.*

*Thatcham*

There are two schemes nationally concerned to improve car security levels, Thatcham and SS/Pact. Thatcham is supported by the Association of British Insurers. It is envisaged that vehicles in our scheme subject to crime for the second time will be protected to Thatcham standards.

*Driveway barriers*

If a car is taken more than once from the victim's driveway, and it is impracticable for the car to be garaged, driveway barriers will be advised, which can be lifted and locked into place while the vehicle is in the vulnerable drive.

**Gold**

*Priority AFR*

Where fingerprints have been lifted at a crime scene they will urgently be conveyed to the Fingerprint Bureau for automated fingerprint recognition (AFR).

*RV used for RIC*

Where the offender is arrested and the offence is a repeat victimisation (RV) that fact may be put before the Magistrates to support an application for a remand in custody (RIC) if there is reasonable suspicion that the same offender was responsible for the earlier offence(s).

*TrakBak*

This is a tracking device enabling items which are taken to be located with relative ease, the system being activated at the moment of its removal. To date, TrakBak is limited to use in vehicle theft. We are urgently exploring the possibility of its extension to car accessories and frequently stolen household items.

*Home Office alarm*

A 'silent' alarm which transmits directly to the Police Control Room and will activate an immediate police response.

*Extended cover by staff (burglary other)*

Victimised commercial operations will be encouraged to extend their own staff cover.

*Laminated windows*

By this means, vehicle or premises windows can be made much less susceptible to breakage from the outside, while retaining ease of breakage from the inside, necessary in case of fire or other emergency. So far used for vehicles only, we are urgently exploring its use for buildings, notably those like schools repeatedly subject to victimisation by the same route.

*Special number plates*

The central part of the number plate is detachable, being removed from the vehicle when it is unattended. If the police see a car being driven with this part of the number plate missing they will understand its likely significance and act accordingly.

*Lease incentive scheme*

This is not yet in place, but the Huddersfield team is currently in touch with BVRLA to discuss incentives to protect leased cars from further victimisation, along the lines of schemes already operating in the Netherlands.

*SOCO*

Vehicle crimes within the 'gold' level will be examined by scenes of crime officers, where the offence falls within the force criteria for such examination.

It is inevitable and desirable that the level and mix of the graded responses will change and develop in the light of experience. Already, it seems clear that the response to theft from vehicles needs boosting at all levels. Protection particular to certain types of premises, notably schools, needs further consideration. We hope to stimulate modifications of equipment to serve novel functions, and are in contact with many manufacturers of security devices.

The unchanging attributes are the fact that the responses are graded, and that 'higher level' responses are geared towards detection.

Current funding for equipment is £40,000 from the Home Office, a sum matched by Kirklees Metropolitan Council. The high-tech options are *loaned* from police stock, so that a limited amount of equipment can be deployed at times of greatest risk, and moved on when risk declines. The more routine changes and the (few) high-tech options which cannot easily be removed must be paid for either by the victim or by the property-owner, if that is different. For example, Kirklees Metropolitan Council is committed to providing equipment to its tenants for domestic burglary prevention. It is currently considering whether it can do so for its community charge payers who are owner-occupiers. The private rental sector is of particular concern. A substantial proportion of this sector comprises tenants who are students at Huddersfield University. The University has pronounced itself willing to act against those landlords who do not agree to improve security after a burglary. Thus action could be to remove such landlords from the list of those approved by the University. The composition of the private rented sector in Huddersfield is being further explored in order to establish other means of persuading private landlords to improve the security of their property.

One of the lessons yet to be learned is the extent to which victims can be induced to take measures of self-protection when they have to bear part or all of the direct cost of so doing. As noted earlier, insurance offers an obvious mechanism for such inducement. In any event, the notion of crisis intervention, that human behaviour is most tractable at times of crisis, suggests that victimisation is potentially the most profitable time at which to persuade people towards self-protective change. How that can be done in a way which does not offend police and victim sensibilities has yet to be determined. It will be one of the points addressed most closely in the second report of the present project.

## Towards implementation

Issues of implementation were also raised by the task groups. About three things there seemed total agreement.

1. Inadequate implementation would vitiate the scheme's merits. This means that there are considerable training implications.

2. The identification of the response level should be made by the officer attending a crime. It should be made extremely simple but the officer should retain some discretion about the response level to be implemented. In short, the default response should be absolutely clear on the basis of a single question to the victim, determining the number of times during the last year that he/she has been victimised in the same way[6]. However, the officer should have the discretion to recommend a level other than the default level.

3. The scheme needs central coordination. Some central person must mobilise the scheme's components and ensure their swift installation and use.

In early September, the staffing of the project was determined. An experienced Detective Sergeant, John Barr, was appointed as local co-ordinator. For its initial three months, a Crime Prevention Officer, PC Steve Bedford, was assigned to the project, to make the visits and recommendations required under the Silver and Gold options. For reasons only partially linked to the project, Huddersfield was chosen to pilot the crime pattern analysis system, and for that purpose, PC Phil Johnson was assigned to help the Divisional Crime Analyst, PC Caroline Sunderland.

### Training

During the week 26th-30th September, two groups of police officers per day were introduced to the project and instructed on their role in it. With a 'mopping-up' session on October 7th, this meant that all officers policing the area knew what was expected of them and why.

6 *There was much discussion about alternative ways of determining this, but they were not regarded as viable, not least because of the problems identified in the data examination stage. This has implications for assessing the level of each scheme type which would be necessary .*

The content of the training comprised:

1. A brief overview of the research on repeat victimisation.

2. A statement of how the approach might help the operational officer. In brief, it was suggested that it helped to focus on the places most liable to victimisation (ie. those already victimised), the times at which they were most liable to victimisation (ie. soon after the prior offence), and the people most likely to be responsible (ie. those detected in offending against the same location in the recent past).

3. A request that officers should ask the victim about prior victimisation, to communicate a crime report swiftly, and to make a recommendation about the level of protection to be offered. Each officer will carry an aide- memoire of the contents of each response level, to guide his or her advice to a victim, and to inform the recommendation of a level of intervention other than the default level for a particular case.

4. The need to get operationally important information about an incident onto CIS quickly, preferably by phoning in from the scene.

**Figure 8: Repeat victimisation aide memoire**

**REPEAT VICTIMISATION**

**Aide Memoire**

Aims:  UP GRADE SECURITY STATUS
DETECTING OFFENDERS

*Without raising the fear of crime in victims*
*Officers should stress:*
**'TOGETHER LET'S MAKE IT MORE DIFFICULT**
**FOR THE CRIMINALS TO STRIKE AGAIN'**

Every first-time offence will receive a BRONZE response which is normally provided by the Officer who attends the scene.

*The following list is to remind Officers of the actions required:*

1. Any previous victimisation in the past 12 months?
2. Crime Prevention advice - postcode property, window locks, etc.
3. Victim Support.
4. Cocoon Watch.
5. Scenes of Crime.
6. Prompt permanent repairs.
7. Prompt CIS recording to include the following information:
  (a)  Are Window Locks fitted?
      Is assistance required?
  (b)  Tenancy Status:  ascertain owner occupied
                       council tenant
                       private landlord.

S/136

**Possible responses from the Co-ordinator**

**SILVER**

Personalised victim letter

CPO visit and advice

'Police Watch' (twice weekly)

Possible insurance incentives

Use of devices i.e. mock occupancy, simple alarm, dummy alarm, audible alarm, etc.

(each officer can make recommendations as to actions suitable in each case).

**GOLD**

Personalised victim letter

Priority fingerprint check

Home Office CP alarms

'Police Watch' daily

Other sophisticated technical devices (i.e. cameras, etc.)

(again each officer is asked to make recommendations as to actions he feels most suitable in this case).

S/136

Discussion after the input was almost universally constructive, considering how the approach would address particular circumstances.

*Media launch*

A media launch of the project took place on November 17th 1994, chaired by the Chief Constable of West Yorkshire Police, Keith Hellawell, and attended by the Minister of State at the Home Office, David Maclean (see figure 9a). The logo and brand-name for the strategy, "Biting Back", were unveiled at the launch and are shown in figure 9b.

*Figure 9a:*
*The media launch*

*Figure 9b:*
*The Biting Back logo*

# 5. Next steps

Administrative help has been promised by Kirklees Metropolitan Council, and Huddersfield University has agreed to contribute a research assistant to look at repeat victimisation of students and its link with residence in private rented accommodation. Manufacturers of security equipment have been approached, and the aspiration of the project is to develop existing techniques into new applications, and to identify market opportunities for novel techniques. Clearly, the time scale for the achievement of this is longer than the year which the project still has to run.

At Huddersfield Police HQ, there is the belief that the projections of the number of multiple victims will be too low. A somewhat plaintive message placed by the project co-ordinator on CIS reads: "Anyone who is still sceptical about whether or not repeat burglaries and car crime exist should contact DS Barr for numerous examples". Because of the approach which was chosen for the level of intervention at the first contact with those victimised in the year before the project began, the early months will be the most hectic and the most resource intensive. This will be all the more so because extra components for the scheme are considered almost daily. Officers, being sensitised to the notion, are identifying repeats from computer and paper records with some frequency, are putting text about these events on CIS, and are visiting the project co-ordinator's office, "all the time". The first arrest attributable to the scheme has been made. Feelings are a mixture of confidence that the approach can work and apprehension that it might not until the practicalities bed down into routine. When one officer asked the divisional crime manager during the training session how long the initiative would last, he replied, "for ever". The task of the next phase of the project is to establish whether or not it deserves to.

## Continuing data analysis

Data gathering will continue throughout the project. The preceding sections have presented some of the data examined so far, and further analysis will be undertaken and documented in the final report of the project.

This will include:

- Further work to establish the level of 'true' repeat victimisation, ie. further checking of the status of those events identified as possible repeats.
- Evaluating the effect of the strategy on repeat victimisation.
- Monitoring the numbers of bronze, silver and gold responses.
- Interviewing victims of non-domestic burglaries and victims of a mix of vehicle crime and burglary.
- Analysis of interviews with victims of vehicle crime.
- Further interrogation of data on the neighbour effect (see below).
- Further evaluation of the link between offenders and victims and the extent to which the same offenders are responsible for repeat victimisations.

*Is it the same offenders?*

Recent analysis of the British Crime Survey has suggested that the bulk of repeated offences of the same kind are similar in method and circumstances, and are presumed by victims to be the work of the same person (Chenery et al. 1994). Offender reports confirm that they do return more often than one would suppose (Winkel, 1991; Gill and Matthews, 1993). The absence of a neighbour effect and the interactions between choice of neighbouring houses reported below point in the same direction. Our next enterprise on these lines will be to look at secondary detections. The frequency with which offenders admit repeatedly offending against the same target, in comparison with the frequency of the same target in the admissions of different offenders, will give a different handle upon the issue.

*The neighbour effect*

The phenomonenon of repeat victimisation suggests that there is something particular about prior victims which makes them suitable targets in the future. Hitherto, the ecological approach has tended to focus on areas rather than individuals as the unit of analysis of crime risk. It is emerging that the effects of prior victimisation are *additive* with area and demographic characteristics (Ellingworth et al. in preparation). It seems that future victims have area *plus* demography *plus* victimisation experience in common. The targeting of prior victims is therefore a shorthand way of targeting those at risk in terms of all three characteristics.

One way of thinking about the point derives from routine activity theory. Routine activity theory requires a motivated offender to be able to identify a suitable target and the absence of a capable guardian. There is clearly a process of selecting a target prior to victimisation, involving, for example, occupancy checks prior to the offence. However, *a motivated offender can only fully identify a suitable victim after a victimisation*. The victim of an assault may show an unexpected aptitude in karate. The dwelling being burgled may house a sleeping Rottweiler. Video equipment may prove to be marked and unexpectedly difficult to remove. If this is true, judgements of victim suitability change *after* an offence. Burglary victims who still have things worth stealing become super-suitable as victims, since they are still worth burgling, and entry and exit points and house layout are known.

If this view is correct, then repeat victimisation should not spread at all. Specifically, if a house is successfully burgled, it will have a high likelihood of re-victimisation. However the neighbouring house should not. The house next door should not incur any increased risk relative to the house next door to it, and to the house next door to that[7].

While these views of repeat victimisation predict the absence of a simple neighbour effect, it does not mean that there will be no links between victimisations of different houses. If there are discernible sequences, this would suggest the same offenders are involved, and that prevention by the detection route is an attractive option.

A study was undertaken to test these hypotheses, full details of which can be found in appendix b. In short, this found that:

1. There is no straightforward neighbour effect. **Immediate neighbours of burgled houses suffer no greater or less risk of being burgled than houses somewhat more distant**. The implications of this are that scheme options should not focus more on the dwelling next door than on other near neighbours in crime prevention (other than as a contributor to a cocoon scheme).

2. **There are substitutive patterns in target selection of nearby houses ie. when burglaries at the same address do not occur, burglaries two doors down are more likely to.** In the writers' view, this is only plausibly explained by the same burglars being involved in enough cases to bring the pattern out. A speculation about this might be that if after a successful burglary the contents prove disappointing, the burglar will target the house

7 *It may of course be that all the dwellings in the street have a higher than average risk of burglary because of the nature of the street.*

most similar in terms of layout and likelihood of being disturbed. If the original burgled house is semi-detached, the most similar one on these criteria will be the house two doors away, rather than next door. Detection-based schemes would thus be promising avenues of very local crime reduction. A tour of Huddersfield is planned to see whether the cases where burglaries occur in the next dwelling but one tend to be semi-detached houses more often than when this pattern does not occur.

## Why should it work?

The importance of specifying the mechanism by which an initiative is hoped to work was noted earlier. These mechanisms are crucial for the proper evaluation of the scheme, in that they define where to look for early signs of change and coincident changes. In the present case, the available evidence indicates that:

1. Repeat victimisation comprises a large proportion of all offences suffered in the area.

2. Repeat victimisation marks out the areas of highest crime rates.

3. Repeats very often occur quickly after a prior victimisation.

4. Repeat victimisations are believed typically to be the work of the same offender.

5. Victimisation increases the risk of future victimisation, rather than merely reflecting risk factors predating the first victimisation.

The defining features of the initiative are graded responses and an increasing emphasis on detection as number of victimisations increases. That being so, the direct effects hoped for are:

1. The deflection of offenders from prior victims who have ceased to be suitable by the introduction of elements of the scheme, like rapid repair/security uprating.

2. The demotivation of repeat offenders by their increased rate of detection.

3.    The prevention of crime by deploying police officers in and around the location of crime at the times when it is most likely to occur.

The indirect effects are hoped to include:

4.    Increased awareness and crime prevention take-up by both prior victims and others.

5.    Changed offender perceptions about the likelihood of any intended target being unprotected. While an offender may not have previously victimised a place or vehicle, he cannot be sure that someone else has not, which would mean that the item in question would be protected, perhaps with a high degree of technical sophistication.

6.    Changed victim and public perceptions of their and the police's potency in controlling crime.

This last point was eloquently elaborated by DCI John Holt in the training sessions of late September. To paraphrase:

"I've been to hundreds of burglaries and I've left wondering - What have I given those people? - I've walked round the garden, looked at the point of entry to seem to be doing something useful, but that's about it. This project gives us a chance of really giving victims something, a real effort to stop it happening to them again, so that they can get on with their lives in peace, which is the reason a lot of us came into this job in the first place."

The feel good factor will not in itself mean success, but its power of motivation should not be understated. It may be the reason why the response of Huddersfield agencies generally has been so positive. As an anecdotal illustration of this, when the officers' aide-memoire for the scheme and the cocoon watch card was taken to a commercial printer, the woman dealing with it spontaneously remarked that the approach was excellent, and she only wished that it had been in place when her mother had been burgled.

# References

**Bridgeman C. and A. Sampson** (1994) *Wise after the Event: Tackling Repeat Victimisation* A report by the National Board for Crime Prevention. London: Home Office.

**Chenery S., A. Tseloni and K. Pease** (1994) "Series Events in the 1992 British Crime Survey" *Paper to the American Society of Criminology, Miami, November*

**Cohen L.E. and M. Felson** (1979) "Social Change and Crime Rate Trends: a Routine Activities Approach." *American Sociological Review 44* 588-608.

**Ellingworth D., D.Osborn, A.Trickett and K.Pease** (forthcoming) 'The Additional Influence of Previous Crime Experience in Models of Victimisation'.

**Farrell G.** (1993) Unpublished Ph.D. thesis, University of Manchester.

**Farrell G. and K.Pease** (1993) *Once Bitten, Twice Bitten: Repeat Victimisation and its Implications for Crime Prevention* Crime Prevention Unit Paper 46. London: Home Office.

**Farrell G., D.Ellingworth, K.Clark and K.Pease** (1994) 'High Crime Rates, Repeat Victimisation and Routine Activities'. Paper to the Cropwood Conference, Cambridge, September.

**Forrester D., M.Chatterton and K.Pease** (1988) *The Kirkholt Burglary Prevention Demonstration Project, Rochdale* Crime Prevention Unit Paper 13. London: Home Office.

**Gill M. and R. Matthews** (1993) *Raids on Banks* Centre for the Study of Public Order: University of Leicester.

**Laycock G.** (1994) "Wise After the Event: Facts and Figures". Paper to the National Board for Crime Prevention Repeat Victimisation Regional Conferences, London, May.

**Lloyd S., G. Farrell and K. Pease** (1994) *Preventing Repeated Domestic Violence: A Demonstration Project on Merseyside Crime* Prevention Unit Paper 49. London: Home Office.

**Mayhew P., N. Aye Maung and C. Mirrlees-Black** (1993) *The 1992 British Crime Survey* Home Office Research Study 132 . London: HMSO.

**Pawson R. and N.Tilley** (1994) 'What Works in Evaluation Research?' *British Journal of Criminology 34 291-306.*

**Polvi N., T.Looman, C.Humphries and K.Pease** (1991) "Repeat Break-and-Enter Victimisation: Time Course and Crime Prevention Opportunity". *Journal of Police Science and Administration 17 8-11.*

**Sampson A. and C. Phillips** (1992) *Multiple Victimisation. Racial Attacks on an East London Estate.* Crime Prevention Unit Paper 36. London: Home Office.

**Tarling R.** (1993) *Analysing Offending* London: HMSO.

**Tilley N.** (1995) *Thinking about Crime Prevention Performance Indicators.* Crime Detection and Prevention paper 57. London: Home Office.

**Trickett A. D.Osborn, J.Seymour and K.Pease** (1992) "What is Different about High Crime Areas?" *British Journal of Criminology 32 81-90.*

**Winkel F.W.** (1991) "Police, Victims and Crime Prevention: Some Research-based Recommendations on Victim-orientated Interventions" *British Journal of Criminology 31 250-265.*

# Appendix A: The time course graph - what does it mean?[8]

The presentation of time course data is fraught with difficulties in both depiction and analysis. In many ways, the time course given in Polvi et al (1991) was the most satisfactory so far used, in that it adjusted for diminishing risk periods, it operated with a long series of data, and it expressed the data as observed / Poisson expected ratios. The problem was that the apparently arcane way of presenting it diminished its impact and credibility with practitioner groups. This is ironic, since it was chosen to avoid being misleading.

The time period for the data here analysed was too short, being below the minimum specified in Farrell and Pease (1993). In what follows, all the figures have been corrected to take account of diminishing risk periods. In an eleven month period (January-November), there are only five months (January-May) when a repeat victimisation six months later would be included in the data set. There are ten months in which a repeat one month later would be included. Without correction, the time course curve is arithmetically bound to go down. The necessary correction[9] has been made in the Figures presented earlier, although the process of correction will amplify random fluctuations in the longer between-burglary intervals. What cannot be corrected for, in these or the figures presented later, is the tendency to under-record repeats generally (see Farrell and Pease 1993). As long as this tendency is independent of time elapsing between victimisations[10], then the shape of the curve would be accentuated, since a similar proportional increase in swift repeats would represent a larger absolute number of repeats.

In figures 2 and 3, presented earlier, the unit of analysis is the burglary event. It shows many swift repeats, with the number declining over time. Thus somewhere burgled on January 1st 1993 and on the first of every month thereafter would contribute ten data points, each in the one-month category. Therefore, the same curve could be arrived at by the frequent victimisation of just a few places or the diminishing probability of repeat victimisation generally with time.

As a description of the distribution of time intervals between events, figures 2 and 3 provide the simplest account of reality from the police perspective. When the phone rings to report a burglary of somewhere victimised earlier, it will most frequently be of somewhere burgled in the very recent past.

8 *We are grateful to Dr William Spelman, Rutgers University, for personal communication pointing out some of the complexities of time-course analysis, and to Denise Osborn, Professor of Social Statistics at Manchester University, for her advice.*

9 *This is done by multiplying the observed number of repeats by eleven and dividing by the gap length. For example, if 40 events with a four month gap were observed, and given that eleven months worth of data were analysed, the adjusted figure would be $(40*11)/(11-4)$.*

10 *We cannot think of any reason for the distant repeats to be less often recorded as such, which would be the only way in which the shape of the curve would not be accentuated. The only plausible reason would be in the opposite direction, with people less inclined to report swift repeats for insurance reasons.*

If some places are so heavily victimised as to swamp the general picture, this is a fact of current life which is reflected in the graph. However, figures 2 and 3 mask the issue of whether any victimised unit tends to be revictimised quickly or slowly.

One way of clarifying the issue is to restrict attention to places which have been victimised only twice in the period in question, so that each place contributes only one data point to the curve. The results of this approach are depicted as figures 10 and 11. It will be seen that the same basic shape is evident as was the case in earlier figures, showing that the time course is not an artefact of multiple counting of the same place. It is clear from this analysis that the conclusion that victimisation follows victimisation swiftly is not an artefact of the presence of the most heavily victimised individuals. Even for individuals suffering only two victimisations, the second tends to follow the first rather quickly.

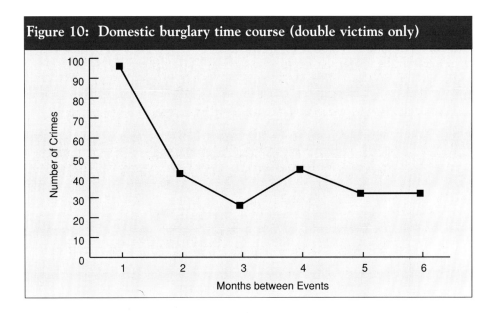

**Figure 10: Domestic burglary time course (double victims only)**

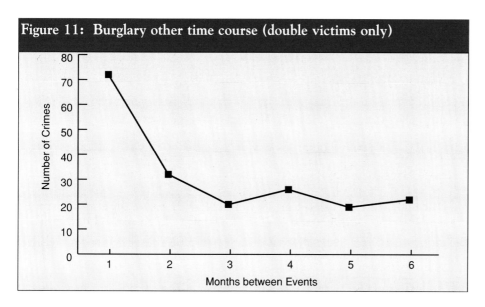

Figure 11:  Burglary other time course (double victims only)

Precisely the same analyses were carried out for theft from and theft/taking of motor vehicles. The time course of all victimisations were presented earlier as figures 4 and 5, and below for double victims only as figures 12 and 13. The same conclusions are merited as for the burglary events - somewhat to our astonishment, given the vicissitudes of identifying repeat vehicle crime, described earlier.

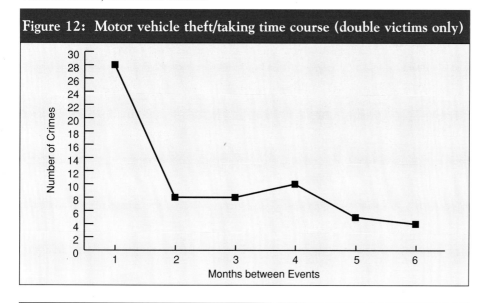

Figure 12:  Motor vehicle theft/taking time course (double victims only)

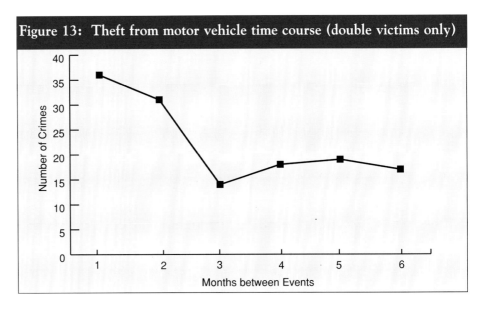

**Figure 13: Theft from motor vehicle time course (double victims only)**

The search for the best way of presenting time course data to combine clarity to practitioners with statistical defensibility continues. The next possibility to be explored when time allows is survival analysis, which is extensively used in the understanding of criminal careers, and which does allow for the optimal use of data sets with varying risk periods (see Tarling 1993). It is important for crime prevention purposes to comprehend the precise nature of the relation of repeat victimisation with time, not least to assess the relative merits of permanent and temporary protection of those repeatedly victimised.

# Appendix B: The neighbour effect

To test the extent to which repeat domestic burglary spreads risk to neighbouring houses, 26 streets in the Huddersfield area which were uniquely named were chosen. All domestic burglary victimisations between June 1st 1992 and July 31st 1994 in those streets were listed on the CIS system. The start date was chosen as being the day on which CIS became operational in Huddersfield. The first burglary in a street was taken as the reference burglary. Let's say 20, Bridgeman St was burgled on June 1st 1992. It was then established whether numbers 18 and 22 Bridgeman St featured on the electoral register, then whether 16 and 24 did so, then whether 14 and 26 did so, and finally whether 12 and 28 did so.

We then looked at burglary experience in the period between June 1st 1992 and July 29th 1994 (the date of extracting the data) at all the dwellings between 12 and 28 Bridgeman St. The process was repeated for the next burglary on Bridgeman St. For instance, if 76 Bridgeman St was burgled on July 8th 1992, all burglaries at even numbers between 68 and 84 until July 31st 1994 were scrutinised, and so on until the reference burglary was the last burglary before June 30th 1993. This means that thirteen months followed the date of the last reference burglary, so that small risk periods were not included. By this means, we reached a total of 218 reference burglaries.

We were then in a position to study victimisation after a burglary, at the same house, the houses next door, two doors away, three doors away and four doors away. Because there were two houses next door (one each side of the house suffering the reference burglary), two doors away, and so on, there should have been double the number of burglaries at each distance than there were repeat burglaries (obviously only the same house's burglary would qualify as a repeat). For this reason the number of repeats was doubled so as to be comparable with neighbour risks.

When only one of the two houses at a particular distance appeared in the electoral register, the number of burglaries at the other house at that distance was doubled to maintain comparability. If both houses at a particular distance did not feature in the electoral register, that reference burglary was omitted from the analysis. One street was eliminated because of possible confusions given that a large number of houses appear to have been knocked together, so that addresses were 48/50, 52/56 and so on. It was after this process of elimination that the total of 218 was reached.

The important aspect of the study was whether there was a pattern around the victimised house, of diminishing, stable or (least plausibly) increasing victimisation. The number of burglaries at each distance is summarised as table 6.

| Table 6. Number of burglaries at varying distances from a reference burglary (see text for details) | |
| --- | --- |
| Distance | Number of Burglaries |
| 0 | 193 |
| 1 | 81 |
| 2 | 70 |
| 3 | 82 |
| 4 | 77 |

It will be seen that there is no systematic change in victimisation among the neighbouring houses according to their propinquity to the dwelling suffering the reference burglary. Statistical testing of that is clearly unnecessary. There is no straightforward neighbour effect. After burglary at a particular house, its neighbours are no more vulnerable than those in dwellings somewhat further away. In contrast, there are many more victimisations at the house already burgled.

Those familiar with the data on risks of repeats will be surprised to find the risk of repeats no higher than it appears in table 6. This is primarily because the reference burglary itself is not included in the above tables. To include it would obviously increase the difference between repeats and other burglaries to more familiar levels, but would not be practically helpful in this context. What table 6 contains is the numbers of potentially preventable burglaries following a burglary at a particular house.

To say that there is no straightforward burglary effect is not to say that there is no pattern of burglaries of surrounding houses after a reference burglary. In other words, if a repeat burglary occurs, does this mean that a burglary of a house next door is less likely to occur? If the house two doors away is burgled, does it mean that a house four doors away is more likely to be burgled? Such patterns may be expected if the burglars of the houses in the street were often the same people. If they were different, there would be no reasons for target selection in relation to a previously targeted house, since for these burglars there would be no previously targeted house!

To look at interactions between burglary locations, the data were dichotomised, so that for each reference burglary there was either burglary or no burglary at a given distance. All possible patterns of victimisation were then reflected in one of thirty-two cells and subjected to a simple log-linear analysis. For example, one cell would contain cases where only the same house had been victimised after the reference burglary, one for the case where no house had been victimised, one where all had been victimised, and so on. Table 7 summarises the statistically reliable terms to come out of the analysis. DIST0 refers to repeats, DIST1 to burglaries of next door neighbours, and so on.

**Table 7. Significant terms in analysis of complex target-selection effects (see text for details)**

| Interaction | df | G-squared | p |
|---|---|---|---|
| DIST0*DIST1*DIST2*DIST3 | 1 | 4.094 | .0430 |
| DIST0*DIST1*DIST2*DIST4 | 1 | 4.228 | .0398 |
| DIST2*DIST3*DIST4 | 1 | 6.479 | .0109 |
| DIST0*DIST2 | 1 | 4.306 | .0380 |
| DIST1*DIST3 | 1 | 3.727 | .0535 |
| DIST3*DIST4 | 1 | 5.673 | .0172 |

It will be seen that there are complex target selection sequences *relative to a burgled house*. The four-way terms seem too subtle for analysis, but the fact they are there at all suggests that the same burglars are involved at least in enough cases to make a pattern visible. The two-way interactions are clearer. For instance the DIST0 * DIST2 term means that repeats and burglaries two doors away are to some extent substitutive. There is a significant inverse relationship, such that when burglaries at the same address do not occur, burglaries two doors down are more likely to. The other two-way patterns are also substitutive, so that either a house three doors down or a house four doors down tends to be burgled, as is the case for the house next door or the house three doors away.

# Crime Prevention Unit Series Papers

1. **Reducing Burglary: a study of chemists' shops.** Gloria Laycock. 1985.
2. **Reducing Crime: developing the role of crime prevention panels.** Lorna J.F Smith and Gloria Laycock. 1985.
3. **Property Marking: a deterrent to domestic burglary?** Gloria Laycock. 1985.
4. **Designing for Car Security: towards a crime free car.** Dean Southall and Paul Ekblom. 1986.
5. **The Prevention of Shop Theft: an approach through crime analysis.** Paul Ekblom. 1986.
6. **Prepayment Coin Meters: a target for burglary.** Nigel Hill. 1986.
7. **Crime in Hospitals: diagnosis and prevention.** Lorna J.F. Smith.
8. **Preventing Juvenile Crime: the Staffordshire Experience.** Kevin Heal and Gloria Laycock. 1987.
9. **Preventing Robberies at Sub-Post Offices: an evaluation of a security initiative.** Paul Ekblom. 1987.
10. **Getting the Best out of Crime Analysis.** Paul Ekblom. 1988.
11. **Retail Crime: Prevention through Crime Analysis.** John Burrows. 1988.
12. **Neighbourhood Watch in England and Wales: a locational analysis.** Sohail Husain. 1988.
13. **The Kirkholt Burglary Prevention Project, Rochdale.** David Forrester, Mike Chatterton and ken Pease with the assistance of Robin Brown. 1988.
14. **The Prevention of Robbery at Building Society Branches.** Claire Austin. 1988.
15. **Crime Prevention and Racial Harassment in Asian-run Small Shops: the scope for prevention.** Paul Ekblom and Frances Simon with the assistance of Sneh Birdi. 1988.
16. **Crime and Nuisance in the Shopping Centre: a case study in crime prevention.** Susan Phillips and Raymond Cochrane. 1988.
17. **The Prevention of Fraud.** Michael Levi. 1988.
18. **An Evaluation of Domestic Security Surveys.** Gloria Laycock. 1989.
19. **Downtown Drinkers: the perceptions and fears of the public in a city centre.** Malcolm Ramsey. 1989.
20. **The Management and Prevention of Juvenile Crime Problems.** Barrymore Cooper. 1989.
21. **Victim Support and Crime Prevention in an Inner-City Setting.** Alice Sampson and Graham Farrell. 1990.
22. **Largerland Lost? An experiment in keeping Drinkers off the street in cental Coventry and elsewhere.** Malcolm Ramsey. 1990.

23. **The Kirkholt Burglary Prevention Project: Phase II.** David Forrester, Samantha Frenz, Martin O,Connell and Ken Pease. 1990.
24. **Probation Practice in Crime Prevention.** Jane Geraghty. 1991.
25. **Lessons from a Victim Support Crime Prevention Project.** Alice Sampson. 1991.
26. **The Prevention of Cheque and Credit Card Fraud.** Michael Levi, Paul Bissell and Tony Richardson. 1991.
27. **Making Crime Prevention Pay: initiatives from business.** John Burrows. 1991.
28. **The Influence of Street Lighting on Crime and Fear of Crime.** Stephen Atkins, Sohail Husain and Angele Storey. 1991.
29. **The Effect of Better Street Lighting on Crime and Fear: a Review.** Malcolm Ramsay with the assistance of Rosemary Newton. 1991.
30. **Reducing Crime on the London Underground.** Barry Webb and Gloria Laycock. 1992.
31. **Assessing Crime Prevention Initiatives: The First Steps.** Geoff Berry and Mike Carter. 1992.
32. **Tackling Car Crime.** Barry Webb and Gloria Laycock. 1992.
33. **Car Theft in England and Wales: The Home Office Car Theft Index.** George Houghton. 1992.
34. **Preventing Car Crime in Car Parks.** Barry Webb, Ben Brown and Katherine Bennett. 1992.
35. **Closed Circuit Television in Public Places.** Terry Honess and ElizabetCharman. 1992.
36. **Multiple Victimisation: Racial Attacks on an East London Estate.** Alice Sampson and Coretta Phillips. 1992.
37. **Theft and Loss from UK Libraries: A National Survey.** John Burrows and Diane Cooper. 1992.
38. **Safer Cities and Community Safety Strategies.** Nick Tilley. 1992.
39. **Community Service and Crime Prevention: the Cheadle Heath Project.** Mary Barker, Ken Pease and Barry Webb. 1992.
40. **Car Crime and Young People on a Sunderland Housing Estate.** Eileen Spencer. 1993.
41. **Developing Police Crime Prevention: Management and Organisational Change.** Valerie Johnston, Joanna Shapland and Paul Wiles. 1993.
42. **Understanding Car Parks, Crime and CCTV: Evaluation Lessons from Safer Cities.** Nick Tilley. 1993.
43. **Kerb-Crawling, prostitution and Multi-Agency Policing.** Roger Matthews. 1993.

44. **The Prevention of Street Robbery.** Mary Barker, Jane Geraghty, Barry Webb and Tom Key. 1993.
45. **The Prevention of Crime Against Small Businesses: The Safer Cities Experience.** Nick Tilley. 1993.
46. **Once Bitten, Twice Bitten: Repeat Vicimisation and its Implications for Crime Prevention.** Graham Farrell and Ken Pease. 1993.
47. **After Kirkholt - Theory, Method and Results of Replication Evaluations.** Nick Tilley. 1993.
48. **Preventing Domestic Violence to Women.** Rebecca Morley and Audrey Mullender. 1994.
49. **Preventing Repeated Domestic Violence: A Demonstration Project on Mersyside.** Sam Lloyd, Graham Farrell and Ken Pease. 1994.
50. **Vehicle Watch and Car Theft: An Evaluation.** Terry Honess, Michael Maguire and Elizabeth Charman. 1994.
51. **Burglary Reduction: Findings from Safer Cities Schemes.** Nick Tilley and Jancie Webb. 1994.
52. **Inter-Agency Crime Prevention: Organising Local Delivery.** Mark Liddle and Loraine Gelsthorpe. 1994.
53. **Crime Prevention and Inter-Agency Cooperation.** Mark Liddle and Loraine Gelsthorpe. 1994.
    **Inter-Agency Crime Prevention: Further Issues** (Supplementary Paper to Crime Prevention Unit Papers 52 & 53.
54. **Crime on Industrial Estates.** Valerie Johnston, Maria Leitner, Joanna Shapland & Paul Wiles. 1994.

## Crime Detection and Prevention Series

55. **Witness Intimidation: Strategies for prevention.** Warwick Maynard. 1994.
56. **Preventing Vandalism: What Works?** Mary Barker and Cressida Bridgeman. 1994.
57. **Thinking About Crime Prevention Performance Indicators.** Nick Tilley. 1995.

# POLICE RESEARCH SERIES PAPERS

1.  **Video Taping Police Interviews with Suspects - an Evaluation.** John Baldwin. 1992.
2.  **Effective Shift Systems for the Police Service.** Richard Stone, Tim Kemp, Bernard Rix and George Weldon. 1993.
3.  **Opportunities for Reducing the Administrative Burdens on the Police.** Paul Cresswell, Graham Howarth, Mike Dolan and John Hedges. 1993.
4.  **Investigative Interviewing Courses For Police Officers: An Evaluation.** Barry McGurk, Michael Carr and Debra McGurk. 1993.
5.  **Management and Supervision of Police Interviews.** Janet Stockdale. 1993.
6.  **Royal Commission Research Papers. A Policing Perspective.** Jane Hirst. 1993.
7.  **Part-Time Working and Job Sharing in the Police Service.** Richard Stone, Tim Kemp and George Weldon. 1994.
8.  **Managing demand on the Police: An evaluation of a Crime Line.** Chloe Jolowicz and Tim Read. 1994.
9.  **Court Attendance by Police Officers.** Bob Eames, Andrew Hooke and David Portas. 1994.
10. **Assaults on Police Officers: An examination of the circumstances in which such incidents occur.** Ben Brown. 1994.
11. **Assessing the Expandable Side-handled Baton.** Egmont Koch, Tim Kemp and Bernard Rix. 1994.
12. **Traffic Organisation and Activity Study.** Adam Ogilvie-Smith, Elizabeth Ransom and Alan Downey. 1994.